The Holy Spirit in Viet Nam

The Holy Spirit in Viet Nam

Orrel N. Steinkamp

Creation House
Carol Stream, Illinois

© 1973 by Creation House. All rights reserved. Printed in the United States of America. Published by Creation House, 499 Gundersen Drive, Carol Stream, Illinois 60187.

Library of Congress Catalog Card Number: 73-86951
International Standard Book Number: 0-88419-068-4

All biblical quotations, unless noted otherwise, are from the *New American Standard Bible* © 1971 by the Lockman Foundation and are used with permission.

Contents

Introduction

When you think of Viet Nam, what do you see?

Panic-stricken, screaming children running naked from a napalm bomb attack that has burned the clothes off their scrawny bodies?

An eighteen-year-old GI crying in frustration while a friend dies in his arms on the floor of a rescue helicopter?

Cold-blooded, on-the-spot executions on a Saigon street?

Agonized Kent State University students, some crying, others staring blankly at the blood oozing from Jeff Miller's body?

The world map, with Viet Nam hanging down like a grotesque, ugly wound from Asia's stomach?

1

Introduction

A black page in American history that shouldn't have happened, that tore families apart until finally the POWs came home and we tried to forget?

I've tried to forget too, but I can't. For I was there in this war-torn hornets' nest and it wasn't pretty.

But I have some other memories as well. For a new thing is happening in Viet Nam. And that is the story of this book. It is not the account of the controversies of Viet Nam, but of the Christ in Viet Nam.

Rev. Thomas Stebbins, chairman of the Christian and Missionary Alliance (C&MA) mission in Viet Nam, summarized its beginnings in his annual report of July 1972:

> The most notable cause for rejoicing this past conference year has been *revival*. . . . Revival fires broke out among the missionaries last conference (May '71) and led to a great purging and empowering for life and service. Many missionaries have testified to being filled with God's Spirit at that time and to experiencing unprecedented blessing in their ministry throughout the past year. . . . On December 3 at the Nha Trang Bible Institute during a class session on the history of revivals, the fires of revival again broke out. For several days students confessed sin and were filled with the Holy Spirit, experienced miracles and witnessed with unusual grace. . . . These students in turn went to many of their home churches and began to testify to the revival spirit at Nha Trang.

I was the teacher of that class.

To some, this book may be disturbing. For of necessity it must include many mind-boggling episodes of the supernatural. Some readers will be uncomfortable in this area and want to demythologize the supernatural in New Testament times as well as in the present.

This book is intended simply to be a factual account. I do not hope to "stir" anyone into any attempt to seek the unusual. The signs and wonders in Viet Nam were not sought; they were brought by the power which God released.

Perhaps some will say, "Tell us about souls saved but spare us the bizarre details of prescientific superstition." But the miracles come with the package, and our New Testament is filled with these same mind-boggling events. In Acts, we read of thousands being "added daily," but also of a fair amount of "signs and wonders": the cripple is healed at the Gate Beautiful . . . Peter in a trance sees a vision . . . Philip preaches and unclean spirits come out of many possessed . . . many lame and paralyzed are healed . . . Paul sees a light from heaven.

Many of the ethnic Vietnamese churches are now trying to assess just what kind of powerful wind it was that suddenly came billowing out of the heavens. Indications are that the tribal (Montagnard) church will be called on to bring the revival back to the Vietnamese church. Reports have come that tribal pastors and leaders are being invited by many large Vietnamese churches in urban areas to share the secret of revival.

This book tells a new story about Viet Nam. I hope you think of that war-torn nation in a different light after reading it.

Part One
One Week in Nha Trang

1

Room 5

December 3, 1971, started like any other day of classes at Nha Trang Biblical and Theological Institute in South Viet Nam. As I made my way to the "History of Revivals" class, I didn't realize that this Friday would be the flash point of a revival which would sweep Viet Nam with such power that a Vietnamese evangelist would eventually report: "The highlands of Viet Nam are aflame!"

The night before God prepared me in a very unusual way. Each Thursday evening I attended a fellowship of Jesus People at the nearby military chapel. During a time of meditation I sensed very clearly in my mind that Christ was telling me He wanted me to include in my ministry two new things: praying for the sick and exorcising demonic influence.

This came as quite a shock. Only a few months before I would have laughed at such a thought. But then, in late fall, I had attended a retreat for soldiers at Cam Ranh and seen a young airman delivered dramatically from demon possession.

On this Thursday night, a serviceman testified that we needed faith to pray for the sick and to cast out evil spirits. I accepted this message of God and commented to my wife that I would simply wait until God put me in a situation where healing or exorcism was required.

Then, suddenly I stopped being an observer and took part in this matter of faith. We all gathered and prayed for a young airman whose father was in a terminal cancer ward in the States. As we left that meeting, we knew the soldier's father would be healed (he was, we found out a month later).

Other missionaries were going through the same experience. That same evening, God laid an unusually heavy burden for revival on the hearts of many of the teachers and workers at the seminary. We were all ready. We didn't know it, but God did.

My class was to start at eleven. Just before class, we discovered that one of the teachers had dismissed his scheduled class for some reason, so the students hurried to invite as many students as possible to come hear the report on revival in Indonesia. Thus when class began, about 55 of the school's 117 students were in Room 5.

A student, Mr. Thien, commenced to give a very thorough account of the recent revival in Indonesia. Especially moving were the accounts of the healings and other miraculous signs.

At the end of the period Mr. Thien made an appeal to pray for revival in Viet Nam to begin at the seminary. For about ten minutes the praying was normal, but then at noon a student began to weep and pray and to confess specific sins. Suddenly the room was alive with spontaneous, simultaneous prayer. Students began to lift their hands to heaven. Pride was set aside and they were all swept into the presence of the living Christ. The presence of the Lord had fallen.

Some students did not attend the meeting and at noon went down to the dining room for the noon meal, only to find that most had not yet come to eat. The weeping and crying out to God gained in tempo, causing the remaining students to come up to the meeting. Many, as soon as they entered the room, were immediately overwhelmed and fell on their knees and began crying out to the Lord to forgive their sins.

One student later told how as he was making his way up to Room 5 he met a student running and exclaiming, "Oh! It's frightening!" This student returned to his room but couldn't rest until he finally returned to join the praying group. Another student related that he had determined not to go up to Room 5. He decided to work on a report. However, as he would try to write his hand was so out of control that he misspelled nearly every word. He, too, came to the room to pray.

At about one-thirty, those who wanted to eat were dismissed. I announced that those who wanted to go should be free in the Spirit to do so and then return to continue praying. I went home for a quick bowl of soup, told some other missionaries what was happening, and returned to find about twenty students quietly praying. I began to wonder if the visitation were already over. I poured my heart out to the Lord, imploring Him to draw all the students back for more prayer.

In about a half-hour the students began to return to Room 5 and suddenly, as a strong wind, the Spirit was poured out again. Students began to seek each other out and confess hatred, cheating, stealing and other things to one another. Students began roaming up and down the aisles to confer with those who were smitten by conviction. Some repented of jealousy. Others confessed to stealing small amounts of money. Still others reported of not paying their tithe. In fact, the child evangelism fund, which was in arrears, later showed an 18,000-piaster balance because of those who paid up back tithe. A student went to his room to get a plastic ruler and return it to its owner.

One student came to see one of the missionaries the next day and confessed to him that once when he had been given money to be used for mission work, he used it for something else. He handed the missionary his watch and told him he had no money, but if he would keep his watch, perhaps by Christmas he would have enough money to pay back the debt and redeem his watch.

It was common to see three or four students locked in a weeping embrace. About this time students started coming to me and two other missionaries, Spence Sutherland and David Douglas, asking us to pray for the filling of the Holy Spirit. After we prayed for them some would stand up, lifting their hands high and saying, "Hallelujah!" Then, spontaneous songs of praise would burst out among the students. This scene was repeated over and over again. Students were at times lined up four and five deep, waiting for us to pray for the Spirit's filling. As students were filled with the Spirit, they began to minister to each other. Rapturous joy caused spontaneous singing accompanied by hand clapping.

It was about this time that Tam, a Koho tribe student from Dalat, came forward and asked to be filled with the Spirit and also to be healed of an acute stomach ailment. Only two days before, I had seen him hunched over in pain, waiting to go to the doctor. Two years before he was forced to leave school because of this same problem and now it appeared that he would have to leave school again. We prayed for the fullness of the Spirit. Then I simply placed my hand on his stomach. "In Jesus' name, we claim healing for this man," I said. He was healed. In fact, the next morning he testified that instead of bland rice water he could eat anything, even hot red peppers!

At about six-thirty the meeting was dismissed for a half-hour as the students went out to eat. At 7:00 P.M. they all returned to Room 5. Students now began to testify, telling of God's forgiveness and their new joy and victory. Inspired perhaps by the "Jesus yells" of the Jesus People, the Chinese students would yell out, "Who can forgive sin?" The other students would respond in a deafening roar,

"Jesus!"

"Who can heal our bodies?"

"Jesus!"

The meeting continued informally, some praying, some singing, others testifying, still others standing up to read a few verses of Scripture or to share the burden of their hearts with others for prayer. Former prayers of weakness were now turned into prayers of hope and encouragement. Some lifted their hands while they sang and others clapped their hands according to the beat of the songs. Never before had they experienced the atmosphere of that night.

Others got up and confessed how they had doubted the reports of revivals they had heard about in other lands. But now, having seen this revival with their own eyes, they trusted all the more in the power of God. Others confessed resentments in their hearts against their fellow classmates.

One girl who had a sad disposition stood up and sang, "Oh, Happy Day" to show the transformation in her heart. She continued to testify how that her sight had been impaired after a heavy siege of hepatitis, but now after prayer she could see clearly and didn't need to wear glasses any longer.

Such words of testimony were often interspersed with the singing of "Spirit of the Living God, Fall Afresh on Me," "The Comforter Has Come" and, most special of all, "He's the Lily of the Valley, the Bright and Morning Star." No one led this meeting. It was strictly led by the Holy Spirit. Nobody wanted to dismiss it. Time passed swiftly. The later the hour, the more awake we felt. Rather than winding down, the joy increased as the late hours approached.

Some of the girls told about physical healings. One girl told about how she asked God for a sign of the filling of the Spirit and suddenly her hands and feet became paralyzed for a time. Another girl was given a great sense of heat all over her body. Still another student told of a healing. In the war he had been shot and the bullet was lodged in his leg. He had limped badly. Now he jumped and danced for joy.

Two Koho tribe students who had long-standing grudges found reconciliation at the Cross and together, arm in arm, they testified to the sweet love of Jesus and new love for each other. The meeting continued until 2:30 A.M.

Finally Mr. Thien stood up to witness. Earlier, before beginning his report on the Indonesian revival, he had written in big letters on the blackboard, "Revival in Indonesia." With great joy and emotion he erased "Indonesia" and wrote "Nha Trang Seminary."

2

The Heritage

C. H. Reeves would have been pleased. So would R. A. Jaffray and the other early Alliance pioneers who came to Viet Nam starting in 1897. They had seen revival in those years as well, especially right after World War I, when the church doubled itself each year. The Tourane (Da Nang) church included converts from the royal family and a famous Confucian scholar.

In nearby Fai Foo a popular actor was converted. In one year of his preaching a thousand people were converted. Like Paul, he was jailed and brought before the governor. He was released, and the governor later confided to a missionary, "He almost persuaded me to become a Christian."

The missionaries entered the southern metropolis of

Saigon in 1918, and phenomonal success attended their proclamation despite fierce persecution. The French did not allow them outside the large cities which were under direct French rule. Nationals, however, fanned out into the outlying areas, God confirming their ministry with signs and wonders and many converts.

E. F. Irwin himself, one of the pioneer missionaries, in his book *With Christ in Indo-China* makes repeated reference to the power of the gospel in the lives of early Christians:

> The Annamese had believed in demons; they still believed in them, but they learned that Jesus had conquered Satan. . . .
>
> They expected interpositions of divine power on their behalf, and they received them. Miracles similar to those recorded in the book of Acts were enacted before our eyes not because of the faith of the missionaries, but because of the faith of these 'babes in Christ' who expected from their newly found Savior greater power than they had thought belonged to their old enemy the devil. . . .
>
> The child of one of the students in the Bible school at Tourane was taken sick. He was unconscious and apparently dead. The father called the Vietnamese pastor, who was led to kneel at the bedside and ask God to raise him up. In a few minutes the boy sat up. Within a couple of hours he was playing outside with other children.
>
> Such answers to prayer were common in the church. There was a time when testimonies at fellowship meetings were all along this line, until the missionaries were constrained to pray that the Lord would make plain to the natives how much more precious were spiritual blessings than these physical deliverances! Scores of converts were first attracted to the church because they saw these evidences of the Lord's presence and power.

By 1927 the work had prospered to the point that the Evangelical Church of Viet Nam organized with its own administrative officers.

Work among the non-Vietnamese tribes of the mountainous interior was also initiated. The first continued efforts to evangelize the mountain people began in 1929 in a French mountain resort area called Dalat. In later decades the gospel was planted among the tribal people near Ban Me Thuot as well.

In 1938 revival came to the Vietnamese church through the ministry of the famed Chinese evangelist John Sung. Very few of the pastors and people who experienced this outpouring of God's Spirit are still alive. A Vietnamese student recently interviewed many of them and came up with some incredible stories of God's power in the church.

In 1936 four students at the Vietnamese Bible Institute, then located in Da Nang, began to pray for revival from four to six o'clock each morning. The prayer group enlarged till nearly the whole student body was praying each morning for revival. For two years their prayer meetings persisted. In 1938 God sent His messenger John Sung. Initially his exuberance and flamboyancy brought a negative response among the Vietnamese, with their exaggerated penchant for Oriental protocol and solemnity.

But in Hanoi, Vinh Long, and Da Nang revival came. Joy and confession of sin marked the meetings. As a direct response to the outpouring of God's Spirit and the instruction of John Sung, each church organized one or more witnessing bands. These became a vanguard of evangelism and have become a permanent institution of the church.

In the passing years these witnessing bands have retained their early form but lost much of the early dynamic. Too many times a few elderly men and women faithfully pass out tracts while the rest of the congregation consider themselves absolved of witnessing responsibility.

The revival of 1938 was a great inflow of spiritual

vitality. God knew it was needed to prepare the church for the trying times of World War II and the Japanese occupation. Some missionaries were able to escape, but many others were interned and not released until after the war.

After the war, missionaries returned to find ruin and hardship. Native Christians had suffered much. More suffering was to come. For almost immediately the French were at war with the Viet Minh guerrillas. Missionary work and the advance of the church continued though under hardship until the exit of the French and the Geneva settlement of 1954. For a few years there was relative peace. During these years, especially 1957-58, there was a massive influx of new missionary recruits. Present missionary leadership is in their hands.

But in 1962, the second Indochina war heated up, with the infiltration of the south by Ho Chi Minh and his agents. With the introduction of modern weaponry to both sides, undescribable suffering and bloodletting has been the lot of the Vietnamese. The amount of death, suffering and assassination can never be recorded, let alone comprehended.

Missionary casualties have been unavoidable during these years. Two Wycliffe Bible translators were killed in a Viet Cong ambush. Three Alliance missionaries were taken captive in 1962 and have not yet been found. The Tet offensive of 1968 took the lives of six Alliance missionaries cut off in the highland city of Ban Me Thuot. Miss Betty Olsen, a C&MA nurse; Henry F. Blood, a Wycliffe translator; and Michael D. Benge, a civilian farm adviser, were taken captive at the same time. When the POW's were released in early 1973, Benge emerged to tell how the other two had died of malnutrition.

Vietnamese Christians and pastors suffered, but always their resilient faith bounced back. Their exploits for God amid the ravages of a war would fill volumes.

The Vietnamese church maintained steady, if not significant, growth. During the war years many new church buildings were constructed and there was the appearance of prosperity. In fact, many American Christians were surprised to hear that South Viet Nam had an evangelical community of nearly 100,000 people.

The war brought not only destruction and mourning. To many it brought new affluence and dazzling consumer products. The combination of war weariness and materialism too often robbed the church of its cutting edge of dynamic life and power in the Holy Spirit.

Petty bickerings and power struggles at times seemed ready to divide the church. All would agree that a stifling spiritual mediocrity had settled down on the church. Second- and third-generation Christians were faithful church members, but many pastors lamented the fact that fewer and fewer had really experienced the new birth.

An ambitious program of simultaneous evangelism and renewal was launched in 1970 calling for complete mobilization of all Christians in the task of evangelism. Hours of training sessions and committee meetings brought into being a program called "Evangelism Deep and Wide." This program was patterned after Evangelism in Depth, so successful in Latin America. During the years when the political future of the country was bleak and the takeover of the country seemed imminent, Rev. Doan Van Mieng, president of the Evangelical Church of Viet Nam, pondered the future of the church. People asked him if he were preparing a contingency plan for an exodus of Christians to some other peaceful spot in Asia. Perhaps this idea was spawned by the constant rumor that the Roman Catholic church had plans to mass-evacuate Viet Nam in the event of a communist takeover.

Mieng struggled before the Lord until peace came to him with the conviction that the church would stay no matter what happened. In addition, God gave him the goal that through the mobilized witness of the church they would seek the goal of ten million conversions.

Although the venture was well planned, still it did not catch fire with the church generally. Now and then certain churches applied those principles of growth, but response was spotty at best.

Into this situation God began to move in power among his people. A new thing was happening. But before the full impact of God's presence could be unleashed, something had to happen first — the missionaries had to be reached and set afire. If the country was to once again experience those great moments so frequent in the 1920s, the thirties and the forties, it had to start with the missionary.

3

What Had to Happen First

"*Supersaints get right.*" That sounds irreverent, but it could describe what had to happen before the revival could come.

All too often a missionary is put on a pedestal. After all, he gives up the conveniences and amenities of the civilized world to live in faraway countries among primitive people and hardship. His dedication appears superhuman; he seems untouched by the spiritual struggles of less dedicated mortals.

Every four to five years he returns with quaint pictures which sometimes rival *National Geographic*; he speaks a strange language and eats exotic foods. All in all, he's unique.

This stereotype places great pressure upon the missionary, for he himself is keenly aware that he too suffers the same temptations and struggles of soul common to all disciples of Christ.

In fact the missionary is exposed to more subtle temptations and stress that are not found in the homeland. All who move into a second culture must experience culture shock. This experience can cause great discouragement; it will in any case bring alarming self-discovery. For many, this leads to depression and spiritual defeat.

But at other times the missionary may unconsciously succumb to the propaganda about his unique spirituality and begin to rest upon his spiritual reputation.

Still others, spurred on by a spiritual hero complex, will throw themselves unsparingly into missionary activity, trying somehow to live up to this image, only to fall eventually into a chronic spiritual tiredness. At times their motivation is not spiritual at all; it comes from personal ego and mere human resources.

It was never intended to be this way. The Apostle Paul labored strenuously indeed, but in Colossians 1:29 he points out his labor stemmed from "all the energy and power of Christ at work in me" (New English Bible).

Serving Jesus and relying on our own human resources, talents, and ingenuity ultimately leads to spiritual fatigue.

Among many of us in the Christian and Missionary Alliance family in Viet Nam, spiritual malaise had set in. We were aware of this, I'm sure, but no one voiced any solutions other than more dedication and discipline to the work of the gospel.

One of our more active missionaries in Saigon suddenly became aware that in all the scurry of missionary activity the spontaneous life of Jesus was somehow becoming less and less evident. The fires of devotion were burning dangerously low. There was little time for prayer, and the presence of Jesus seemed distant and strangely unnecessary.

He recalls,

> I had been passing through a desert experience for almost a year. The wells seemed to have dried up. . . . Frustration and disillusionment harassed my mind and I concluded that I was a casualty. But then I reminded myself that in Christian leadership there is no place for casualties. We are all to be victors. This only added to my frustration. For seven years an intense and successful ministry had been carried out. But something was wrong. The program was now too much for me. What I was doing was good and valid, but *how* I was doing it seemed all wrong. I had thought that what I was doing was so important that I had foolishly sacrificed what I needed most — my spiritual well-being, my physical health and my family. Nothing had been withheld, the task came first, the gospel must be gotten out before it was too late. So I worked and ministered and promoted and ran and ran until I ran myself into the ground, until I was a casualty at my own hands! The program was a great success, but I had paid a terrible price.
>
> I knew that something had to be done if I were to recover. I knew I had to extricate myself from much of the work and involvement. So I proceeded to schedule a withdrawal so that in the shortest possible time I would be free from many of the administrative burdens I had carried. I wanted to be free, free to seek God; for there was a growing conviction deep in my heart that my only hope for spiritual renewal was a fresh baptism of the Holy Spirit.

In desperation this man and his wife decided to drastically cut back their activities and seek to know the spontaneous life of walking in the fullness of the Spirit of Christ. They began to fast and pray and search the Scriptures each day during the midday siesta. On this same compound lived three other missionary families, and one by one they joined the midday prayer fellowship. Week by week the quest continued and thirst mounted. Months passed, and then God answered their cries and filled their hearts to overflowing with the fullness of the Spirit of Christ.

The annual field missionary conference was fast approaching. Each year all the missionaries leave their stations and gather for about a week of discussion and business. There are also planned social activities. Beyond this each year are included special services with an invited speaker in which the missionaries give time to warming spiritual fires and prayer.

I hardly expected anything above the normal at this conference. God, however, wanted to refresh people and sent Rev. William Allen from Mansfield, Ohio, to minister. In addition, an Alliance missionary from neighboring Thailand was suddenly constrained to fly to Saigon, not at all aware of the purpose. He arrived unannounced at the mission compound where the months of prayer had preceded. His ministry among us was obviously anointed by the Holy Spirit.

As the missionaries arrived on the compound, revival broke out among them and they experienced the joy of spiritual refreshment and the anointing of the Spirit of God in praise and victory. The gifts of the Spirit were manifest.

From there the revival moved to the conference meetings. Impromptu nights of prayer and testimony were called. Misunderstandings were aired, new joy and power continued on into the evening hours. Many missionaries gave testimony to being filled with the Spirit of God.

Thus the Holy Spirit moved first among the missionary staff. But the movement of the Spirit now begun was not just for missionaries. It was destined to extend far beyond them.

A new atmosphere of love and sharing together as the Body of Christ came to the families stationed at Nha Trang — the Sutherlands, the Douglases and us. In addition, two families, the Paul Collinses and Dr. and Mrs. Green were living in the city.

Previously, each Tuesday evening the station prayer meeting had been held. A spirit of unity and camaraderie had always existed, but now there came a new sense of love and concern for each other so that we began to meet for prayer and spiritual sharing three times a week. Sometimes whole mornings were given to prayer and fellowship.

4

A Beachhead

Where would we go from here? We wanted to see revival in the Vietnamese church. However, as we prayed it seemed as if nothing at all was stirring among the nationals.

But God had other plans. He shifted the revival to the GIs stationed in the area.

Some months previous two or three GIs started what later became known as the "Thursday Evening Power Hour." From humble beginnings God now began to move. One GI who knew he was a Christian but who was timid in witnessing took a two-week furlough in the States. Here he came in contact with the Jesus Movement on the beaches in Florida. He came back fired up and bold to witness. It wasn't long until there were many conversions.

In Nha Trang were stationed thousands of Army, Navy, Air Force and Marine military personnel. One whole section of Nha Trang's beautiful tropical beach on the South China Sea was cordoned off for U.S. military use. Here with an unending supply of scantily clad Vietnamese prostitutes, booze and barbequed steak, the GIs washed away their homesickness and boredom.

With the encouragement of a Spirit-anointed chaplain, Daniel Davis, a beach rally was planned. It featured guitars and singing, and testimonies from those only recently converted and delivered from hard drugs. Some weeks later at this same beach, with people standing around, two young men were baptized. Many GIs and friends came up to ask these new converts about their faith. A beachhead was about to be established.

Nha Trang also had a U.S. military drug rehabilitation center. Here scores of GIs who had become addicted, especially to heroin, were given a two-week drying-out period.

The "Jesus Boys" were allowed to come on Sunday afternoons to speak to the addicts. I personally heard them tell of some "thirty-second heroin cures" by prayer, but it wasn't till some weeks later that I personally saw the power of God revealed at this drug center.

The afternoon I joined the group there were about four GIs and a chaplain. We began the meeting with informal guitar singing followed by a testimony from one of the GIs. Suddenly one of the addicts, a Mexican-American, interrupted with:

"Hey! Man, while you were telling about Jesus I suddenly felt something like a cold wind blow over my body, and then it seemed like all the sin and evil of my life poured out of my whole body like sweat, and now I feel clean. I guess I must be saved or whatever you call it."

A soldier next to him suddenly came to life. "Man!

That's what I need. I used to go to Sunday school, and I've tried many times to open my life up to Jesus, but every time I do it seems all despair and darkness."

He had hardly stopped talking when yet another addict spoke up:

"Last night I came to this very room and I asked Jesus into my heart and now I know that my sin is forgiven and I belong to God. But I have heard that there is an experience called the baptism in the Holy Spirit.

"I need this power — does anyone around here know anything about this?" Quickly one of the soldiers assured him that if he stayed after the service, he could receive this.

After a few more songs, the meeting broke up. We started counseling with the second young man. He seemed eager to get to the point of personal prayer for salvation. He bowed his head, but he did not pray. I coached him firmly that he must verbally pray and invite Jesus into his life, but nothing would come out. Then he said, "It is all despair again. I can't pray."

Some months before this I would have been stymied at this point. But because of another experience I had witnessed in which a demon was exorcized from a young airman who also couldn't pray to receive Jesus, I now sensed that there was an active opposition in his life over which he personally had no control. I called over some of the other Christians and we decided to pray for deliverance from demonic opposition.

All the GIs gathered around and in the name of Jesus Satan was rebuked. We demanded that all demonic influence be cast from him.

The young man began to tremble and appeared unable to speak. A struggle of a few minutes ensued in which we repeatedly stated the authority of Jesus over the demon. Suddenly he slumped into relaxation and then began to extol the beautiful name of Jesus. Obviously he was not aware of any of us in the room as the presence of Jesus flooded his being.

About this time the young man who had asked about the baptism in the Holy Spirit jumped up and said, "Hey! Don't forget about me." We asked him to sit in a chair and all the Christians laid hands on him. Suddenly his body flexed as if shocked by an electric surge. After a few seconds he also quietly began to offer praise and extol the name of Jesus.

About this time the Mexican-American soldier was asked if he wanted to be filled with the Holy Spirit. "Sure! Why not? If God has this gift for His children, I don't want to pass it up." He sat in the same chair and the same GI Christians prayed for the filling of the Holy Spirit. I was surprised when suddenly this man too seemed to receive something like a shock into his body. He too was lost in praise, oblivious to his surroundings.

Still our hearts yearned for revival blessing among our national colleagues and especially at the seminary where we taught. Unknown to us, God had already begun to prepare a man to be a forerunner to revival. Rev. Truong Van Tot had for many years been a Vietnamese missionary to the Koho-speaking tribal church located near the mountain city of Dalat. (*Koho* is actually a loan word from the Cham language meaning *barbarian*. There are seven different tribes or dialect groups in the Dalat area: Sre, Reong, Lac, Chil, Ma, Tring and Rog Lai. One person speaking one dialect can be understood by all.)

Tot had heard of the great revival in Indonesia while he was attending Fuller Theological Seminary's Institute of Church Growth. God met him in a special way, and he wrote letters to many in Viet Nam asking forgiveness for things in his life. When he returned to Viet Nam he nursed a deep desire to see revival among the people he ministered to, namely the Koho tribal church. This tribe had a great Christian heritage, but discouragement and a return to fetishism had pulled down the spiritual level.

As September approached, I contemplated the new school year. I longed for revival, first at the school and then within the whole church. The Evangelism Deep and Wide program hadn't generated all that much fervor. Some church leaders backed it strongly while others simply gave nodding approval and carried on the normal church life and activities. Revival seemed the only hope to awaken a church to its God-given mandate of evangelism.

The thought crossed my mind that I should teach a course on major revivals in church history. When I suggested this to the Vietnamese academic dean, he only replied that this was not a normal course. However, at a faculty meeting I asked President Huyen. He approved. Then, so did the academic dean.

During the first weeks, I taught the scriptural basis for revival. I was immediately aware that the students had returned from their student pastorates with a hunger for revival and an outpouring of God's Spirit.

"We've met so much indifference and opposition," one said.

"Unless God sends spiritual power, I won't remain in the ministry," said another. They were keenly aware of the church's desperate need for spiritual renewal. After about a month, I assigned each student a research project on the various revivals for which I had material.

Tran Cuong was the first to report. He reported on the charismatic movement in the Catholic Church, using material from the book *Catholic Pentecostals.* Viet Nam has many Catholics, and the Evangelical Church has always been estranged from them, especially during the presidency of Ngo Dinh Diem. As

Tran Cuong reported about the deep work of the Holy Spirit among these Catholic people the students recognized that God was doing a new thing.

The next week Nguyen Van Hue gave a report on the 1970 revival at Asbury College in Kentucky. His material was from Robert Coleman's book *One Divine Moment*. Interest in revival became evident.

The following week Ha Minh Vinh gave a report of Dr. John Sung's revival in the church of Viet Nam in 1938. Although we were all aware of this revival, nothing was in print about it. Mr. Vinh researched his subject by interviewing some of the retired pastors who had experienced this revival. A few minutes before class, some of the fellows passed the word to students with free hours and the result was that the classroom was bulging with students. Vinh's report was excellent, and it brought revival into Vietnamese terms. Many students had only heard vaguely of this revival, and when the accounts of healings, conversions, and confession of sin were given there was an obvious presence of the Holy Spirit.

During this time the Seminary Missionary Union invited Truong Van Tot from Dalat for a missionary conference. God greatly used him, and many Vietnamese students offered themselves to take the gospel to tribal mountain people still unreached. Among his messages he gave an account of the revival that came to Indonesia. This created interest in the power of God and the miraculous.

The following Sunday evening, Bob Rogers, a young man sent by Teen Challenge to work with the U.S. military on drug problems, came and spoke to the students. Bob told of smuggling Bibles into Russia and Eastern Europe. Mr. Toan, the Vietnamese dean of students, recounted later how he felt that revival was apparently ready to burst at the close of this meeting. The student who led this service, however, was not sensitive to this and simply moved into a question-and-answer time.

About one week before this meeting some fifteen students from the revival class plus a few others began a special prayer meeting for revival at five o'clock each morning. Many said after December 3 that even though they prayed earnestly they really didn't believe an outpouring of God's Spirit would come so soon.

As I said, there was no special reason to expect anything unusual that Friday. However, we weren't the only ones involved.

On the same day, the C&MA leaders in Key '73 were meeting in Chicago.

And an all-night cottage prayer meeting was going on in London, praying for world revival. December 3 was given to prayer for revival in Viet Nam.

In fact, so much prayer had been going on. So many new things had been happening. So many hearts had been presented openly to the Lord. That first day should have seemed like the most normal thing in the world.

Some of us were hesitant to leave for fear that it would not keep going.

But there was much more ahead.

5

Saturday, Sunday . . .

Saturday was the normal day for all the students to go out and witness. By Saturday afternoon, December 4, at about two o'clock, students began to return telling of new authority in witnessing. One girl reported two hundred conversions in one school.

All afternoon, Spence Sutherland, Dave Douglas, and I prayed with students for the filling of the Holy Spirit. Students would take us in adjoining classrooms to pray. When finished with one student we would open our eyes to see two or three students kneeling, waiting for prayer.

About four o'clock one student, a tribal boy from Pleiku, was brought to me. He was unable to pray and said he just didn't have any response to the awakening.

After much counsel it became known that in his family they had worshiped the spirit of rice for many years. Finally he was brought before the group. One of the students had him kneel and pressed him to confess his known sin. He confessed that he had only believed in Jesus intellectually and then prayed to be born again. He confessed a spirit of doubt in God and the Bible.

Another student invited me to pray that the evil spirit which was oppressing him would be bound. Remembering how God had asked me just two nights before to include this in my ministry, I stepped out in faith and in Jesus' name commanded this evil spirit to be taken away. He was released and stood, asking everyone to be quiet while he sang the hallelujah refrain as a solo. Great joy and victory filled the room to see this demonstration of the power of Jesus' name.

One girl who was waiting outside at this time came up to the room to call some of the others to go to an appointed witnessing class. When she entered the room, she saw that all the students were crowded around the front. As she turned away from the room to go teach, suddenly she was aware of sins in her life. She also was keenly aware that if she did not confess these sins, this other student might not be delivered from demonic oppression. Confessing her sins, she continued on her way and taught her children's class with great results. Upon returning to the campus she bounced eagerly up the stairs.

"What about that student?" she asked the first person she saw.

"He has already been delivered!" She broke out in spontaneous praise.

Sunday morning began about six o'clock with early prayers and testimonies. At 8:30 students made their way to the campus chapel for morning worship. Each month, one Sunday morning service is given to testimonies and so this Sunday there was no scheduled preaching.

The president, academic dean, and others were present. Spence Sutherland, who was the leader, explained from Scripture the idea of raising hands in worship in order to clear up any misunderstanding on the part of the faculty, for this is not part of the worship tradition of the Vietnamese church.

At this point a student, Nguyen Yuan Tin, was greatly moved to come and make a call for still-unconfessed sin. Immediately there was a response of about fifteen students. With great brokenness some confessed the sin of adultery.

In normal times, one can debate about the wisdom of public confession of sin. But when the Holy Spirit descends upon a group of people in conviction, one dare not interfere. It would have been impossible to tell these penitents to stop confessing their sins out loud, for the Spirit of God was in command.

Confession and testimony continued until noon. The meeting closed with the president encouraging the students but also suggesting moderation.

Sunday afternoon was free time. Some students studied for a theology test on Monday. Three or four students, however, went down the hill to the local church called Vinh Phuoc. Zealous and aglow with the Spirit, the students began to witness of the revival in the young people's meeting. Suddenly the pastor broke into tears and prayer. He confessed that he had never thought revival could come to Viet Nam. Almost simultaneously the church young people began to weep and confess their faults and sins. The meeting then carried on until eight-thirty. Many young people confessed openly to stealing bicycles, chickens, and other items.

While this church was experiencing revival, a Vietnamese hoodlum was walking past on the road. He heard the weeping and praying in the church. Out of curiosity he walked in. Soon a heavy sense of guilt swept over him and he accepted Jesus as his Savior.

Meanwhile, about a half-mile away at the seminary, a Sunday evening meeting of praise and testimony began. We heard the Vinh Phuoc church young people coming up the hill to the school, singing the hallelujah refrain. They came into the meeting and testified and sang for about two hours.

The hoodlum, just recently converted, came to the meeting and was asked to testify. He told of his life of stealing, drug traffic, kidnaping Vietnamese girls into prostitution, and hosts of other sins. Then he exclaimed, "Though my sins were as scarlet, now they are white as wool." This brought great rejoicing and praise.

Finally, at about midnight, the meeting came to a reluctant close. We had no doubts but that the revival would continue. We wondered: "Where next?"

6

Singing Hallelujah in Theology Class

The question was soon answered. God wasn't finished at all. Classes were resumed on Monday morning as usual. But the status quo was gone. The students had given themselves completely to the revival and they marched into their theology exam singing the hallelujah refrain!

In the afternoon at three-thirty my Hebrew class turned into another prayer meeting. Suddenly I was called out of class by Tran Cuong. Another student, Bien, had been very sick with cramps and vomiting all day and had come to Tran Cuong's room. Very definitely the Lord spoke clearly to him, instructing him to "go call the missionary."

Coming to the room, I found Bien with his head on the table. He asked me to pray. I was suddenly moved very much by the entire situation. After praying I asked how he felt. He then told how that as I prayed he could feel the pain leave him in successive stages till it was all gone. Again I was reminded of the previous Thursday when God had asked me to include praying for the sick in my ministry.

Dave and Helen Douglas, along with their servant, began to pray for their helper's young son who was out in a student pastorate. About noon, he suddenly appeared. His mother had advised him to go up to the seminary to see the revival. Shortly he was pouring out his soul in confession. Actually, he had left his church totally demoralized, planning never to return. In his despondency he had lost his desire to serve the Lord and had simply lived off the remaining Christians. During the evening meeting he witnessed to the students of his revival experience earlier that day.

The previous Saturday morning some of the students and Mr. Toan had sent a cable to FEBC radio station in Manila telling of the revival. At 6:30 P.M. Monday it was broadcast to all of Viet Nam. Mr. Toan taped the broadcast and at the 9:30 testimony meeting he played it for the student body. This was a source of encouragement in the Spirit.

At the 9:30 meeting on Tuesday, about thirty-five orphans and Miss Binh, a Vietnamese social worker, arrived from the nearby orphanage. Some of the orphans had attended the young people's meeting at Vinh Phuoc Church. On Monday and Tuesday revival had spread among the 250 orphans. Monday evening the orphans wept and prayed their way to revival blessing. No one led them; they simply came to Miss Binh and asked her to pray and hear their confessions. Many became Christians for the first time. Miss Binh and the orphans sang and testified of their spiritual awakening to the entire student body.

Wednesday morning Mr. Toan met with the District Evangelism Deep and Wide Committee to tell the six ministers from the surrounding area about the revival. The men were so moved that they made a special trip over to the campus to observe and also to invite students to come to their churches on the next Sunday.

The student who had studied the Asbury College revival had read of one person who had tape-recorded on the spot everything that happened. So he had done the same from the very beginning meeting on Friday. The idea was to put it in mimeograph form and send it to churches or areas.

Near Nha Trang is a tribal resettlement village called Suoi Dau. Here Koho and Rag Lai montagnards have escaped the Viet Cong who have driven them from the mountain homeland. Friday evening, December 10, three of the Koho tribe students made their way to Suoi Dau to spread the revival fire. A meeting began at seven o'clock and God's Spirit fell again in mighty power among the tribal people of this village. Deadly enemies made their peace. Confession carried on into the night.

At one point two adults testified that as one student called for repentence, fire appeared to project from his mouth. The people of the village received a great spiritual awakening.

Saturday morning I boarded an Air Viet Nam jet for Saigon. Every six weeks I went to Saigon to teach one week in an extension school of the seminary. On Monday evening I was asked to report to the Saigon missionaries on the revival. Many had received only scant news about it. I spoke about forty-five minutes, and we went to prayer.

As the meeting was nearly over, Garth Hunt asked for prayer for his body. This led to an older woman asking for prayer for stomach ulcers.

Next, a GI Christian came to the front and began to pour out his heart to the Lord, confessing spiritual pride. At one point he shouted out, exhorting everyone to confess any sin in their lives. This brought an added solemnity to the group. Then a tribal boy, who turned out to be the older brother of the tribal boy at the school who was delivered from the rice spirit, came sobbing to the front. We prayed with him, but he received no peace from God. Suddenly he told how his skin on his arms had no feeling. He began to tremble. Stan Lemon and all of us gathered around recognized this as demonic involvement. In Jesus' name we cast out the demonic influence. He was graciously delivered. That night he sang songs of praise long into the night, and the next day went out on the streets to witness voluntarily.

There were two teen-age girls, children of missionaries, who came weeping to the front confessing many specific sins in their lives. The flame was spreading. It would burn brighter yet.

God was still in Viet Nam!

Part Two
Snapshots of Revival

How can I describe an ignition of the Spirit that began happening everywhere almost at once? By the time I left for Saigon, students were already traveling on the weekends to share the revival with nearby churches. The two-week Christmas vacation turned these young firebrands loose to set blazes in all directions. By the time 1972 dawned, we knew that this was not just an emotional binge. A genuine, long-lasting surge of the Spirit had come to the bloody, chaotic country of South Viet Nam.

Perhaps I can best convey what it was like through the following vignettes:

• On December 10, three students left the school for a weekend of ministry. In a series of churches there was almost without exception remorse for coldness of heart and confession of specific sins. God graciously brought revival to the churches of Song Cau, Phu Phong and Quin Hon.

In Quin Hon a service that began at 9:30 A.M. continued on into midafternoon as people and pastor met God.

• The first student to go out was Ha Minh Vinh. He went reluctantly, but with complete assurance that God was leading him. The Spirit spoke to him: "Why don't you return to your home church of Phanrang?" He was frightened. What if he were to return and the church would not allow him to speak at the meeting? He told the Lord that if the school headmaster would grant him permission to go home, he would go. To Vinh's surprise, he was given permission without even a question.

Vinh came to his church just in time for the Sunday morning service. He soon learned that the church was embroiled in a controversy over whether to sell the present church building in order to finance a new building or to remain at the old location and build there. The division was so great that the congregation could not even elect a chairman for the business meeting.

In this charged atmosphere Vinh began to speak of the revival. God granted great authority to His word. Suddenly people began to weep, to stand up and confess their sin. People at odds sought each other out and made reconciliation in sobs and tears. Soon they were embracing each other, something quite strange to Eastern reserve. In this new atmosphere, they began to raise money so they could erect a new building without selling the present church. People began to offer things like Hondas and soldier's pensions. In fifteen minutes, 280,000 piastres ($1,018) were pledged.

• The revival fires began to move to tribal churches. The link with the initial revival at the Nha Trang seminary were the five Koho tribal students.

They did not know when they traveled to Suoi Dau that God had already begun to work among the 799 Christians who lived there. Rev. Truong Van Tot, in his Vietnamese account of revival among the Koho church, stated that Pastor Xieng of the Da Nham church had already reinstituted prayer groups for revival.

In one such prayer group they prayed for a man long sick and he was healed. Their faith was strengthened on December 10 when they prayed for a Mrs. K'Ba who was hemorrhaging and near death. After prayer the hemorrhaging slowed and the next day completely stopped. Tot later wrote that it was actually while they were praying for Mrs. K'Ba that the tribal students from Nha Trang arrived. The students related the outpouring of the Spirit on December 3; at the conclusion thirty girls confessed sin.

• During the Christmas season revival broke out in epidemic proportions among Koho tribal Christians at Dalat. Mr. Tot and Helen Evans, veteran Alliance missionary, were the primary witnesses of this great movement.

The news of revival at the Nha Trang seminary as well as the refugee settlement of Suoi Dau caused all the pastors in the Dalat area to hunger for a similar visitation. They hoped that the five Koho students could come back and share the news of revival. Each of the five went to various churches: Kar returned to Suoi Dau resettlement village; Wan and Bieng to Dalat and Dame; Tam to the Yo Monang area and K'soi to Di Linh.

On the afternoon of December 21 Bieng and Kar went to the Kondo Dame church. Historically, this is one of the first churches among the Koho and has produced many pastors. In 1960 the church divided into two groups: Kondo Dame and Kondo Dangja. Mr. Tot reports:

> The spiritual level of these two churches had declined greatly since the division and there was a feeling of dislike among them.
>
> Rev. Ha Chu of the Kondo Dame church was chronically sick (perhaps tuberculosis) and was very discouraged because the people would not cooperate with him and help build a new church. So he was planning to quit the ministry.
>
> The young people of his church were greatly influenced by the world and wearing hippie pants, with long hair and beads. Their young people had also reverted to keeping Cambodian fetishes, drinking cheap liquor, and practicing other known sins.
>
> On the night of December 21 just these young people assembled to hear Kar and Bieng speak about revival in Indonesia and at the Nha Trang seminary. The Holy Spirit descended in what by now was a very normal way.
>
> The young people began to weep and tremble in the presence of the Lord. They confessed their sin. The session lasted until 3:00 A.M.

Wan and Bieng remained at Kondo Dame to continue to lead the young people and also those who had not as yet met the Lord. The weak and cold Christians came to the church and confessed their sins. From the twenty-third to the twenty-eighth in the Dame church, 208 people made public confession of sin — men, women, and children. The church met around the clock. The pastor later reported that on January 1 there were only fifteen people in the whole church who had not been touched in the revival.

When revival came, the pastor was healed instantly. His face now sparkled with God's glory. He ministered in the power of the Spirit. All his children repented of their sin.

His oldest son had fallen away from the Lord and used a Cambodian fetish for over five years, plus becoming a sorcerer who taught other young people sorcery.

His youngest son, Sau, 12, after his experience of revival, returned to the student hostel where he studied and spoke to all the students of new spiritual life. Twenty-three students confessed their sin. One girl student gave up a fetish and four others were healed instantly in answer to the students' prayer. The four healed were: 'Ben, of vomiting; Ger, of asthma; Ang and Krang, of malaria and headaches.

Another young man named Jrang had fallen away from the Lord for many years. He had become so violent that everyone was afraid of him. When all the other promising young men of Dame had died in the war during Tet 1968, he was very sad and grew long hair and a beard. When revival came, many people began to pray for him, but he was not moved one bit. On the afternoon of December 26 as Wan shook his hand to say good-by to return to Bible school, Jrang surprised everyone with: "You are leaving and I have not received any blessing?"

Wan immediately prayed for him. Suddenly Jrang began to tremble violently like someone out of his mind. It seemed there was a spiritual battle between God's Holy Spirit and the spirits of darkness going on in his body.

He suddenly became very, very strong and began to destroy things. No one could restrain him. As he was jumping around, he thrust his arm through a window. He was cut deeply and blood began to flow like water. It hurt so much that he regained his composure and cried out, confessing his sins and asking God for a miracle. "Stop the bleeding! Bring the wound back together again! If you are really God and love me, show your love right now!"

The other young people gathered around him and prayed in this same way. Instantly the blood stopped flowing and the wound came back together again. Then he slipped into unconsciousness. When he regained consciousness he went to the church and made total confession of his sin. He was changed and began to witness for the Lord to his people. Now he is serving the Lord in the church. He offered a Seiko wrist watch with a value of 13,000 piastres to help build the new church. Before, he had promised to help, but had not paid his promise.

Mr. Doi, a weak Christian, was a member of the Regional Force to protect the village but was always drunk and never attended church. One night after revival had come, as the church gathered in prayer, Mr. Doi's sentry duty put him only thirty meters from the church.

He suddenly seemed to feel the ground around his trench move like an earthquake. Fearing his trench was going to collapse, he jumped out and went home.

His curiosity drew him back, and the same quaking occurred a second time. He ran, panic-stricken, to the church and saw many people inside praying. But he did not go in. It seemed as if some power held him back.

He returned to the trench and the quaking returned. He returned hurriedly to the door of the church. This time he knelt down and prayed. Then he was able to go in and pray with the Christians. He felt that all his sin was put away, and great peace came to him. Since that time till now he is living a totally new life. He does not drink anymore and is a strong Christian.

Mrs. K'Srang had a one-year-old son who had a severe case of diarrhea and was near death, evidently from dehydration. She brought her son to the church for prayer and the child was immediately healed. On Christmas Day, 1971, Mrs. K'Srang, as she was going along the road, heard someone singing the hallelujah revival chorus (seven hallelujahs and an amen.)

She turned around, but she saw absolutely no one and was startled. Suddenly she heard an eerie voice: "Wor (her husband) has not yet repented. Tell him to make haste to repent."

She returned home to relate this to her husband, who had long been a nominal Christian, but who was often drunk and in sin. He immediately went to the church, repented and experienced great, radiant joy.

This was not an isolated phenomenon. Mrs. K'Srang was among ten people in the church at Dame, including Rev. Chub, who heard singing either in church at early morning prayer meeting or along the road to the fields. Yet, "no one" was there.

Mrs. K'Brong, 40 years old, overslept on December 27 and did not go to early morning prayer as usual. In her sleep, a man in a white garment appeared to her and told her to get up and go. She awakened and saw no one but proceeded to go and join the others who had filled the church for prayer. It was about 5:00 A.M. As she approached the building she saw a light like a torch shining upon the cross which stands at the peak of the roof.

On December 28, the Dame church was scheduled to go to the Dangja church for a joint meeting. Mr. Ha Bieng, 40, became very sick with diarrhea. He took medicine but to no avail.

Many people counseled him to go to the hospital but Mr. Bieng was determined to trust God for healing. After the church gathered and prayed for him, they lifted him into a car to go to Dangja to the meeting. He was even more weak. Then a group of young people gathered around him and sang hymns and prayed for him. Before the car arrived at Dangja he was completely well. He went to the meetings and later feasted with the Christians in perfect health.

Many others were healed instantly and completely delivered from their afflictions after the church prayed for them. For instance, Mrs. K'Pho, who had tuberculosis, was healed. K'Phet, four years old, the son of Mr. Ka On, who had chest pains for three months, was healed December 28. Ha El, two years old, the son of Mrs. K'Bai, who had had a malaria attack for seven days, was instantly healed on December 22. Mrs. K'Soi, who suffered for five years, was healed in answer to prayer December 12. Mrs. K'Wieng was healed of asthma. Mrs. K'Trang, who could not walk because of defective knees, was healed. Mrs. K'Brong, who was hemorrhaging blood from both her mouth and ears, was immediately healed as the church prayed for her. Both Mrs.

K'Bing and her three-month-old baby had been very weak. She was restored instantly to good health, and her child was quickened at the same time. She was the lady who heard the praise singing her way to the village of Lenkhung.

Mr. Krong, after he had come to the church early one morning to confess sin and pray, was aware of a strange pleasant odor. He also heard someone singing the praise song in the church, even though he was the only person in the building.

Mr. Hon and Sung had been holding a grudge for ten years. In the revival, they confessed their hard feelings and expressed love to each other.

Those who had robbed God of tithes paid their back tithes, some four to five times more than the original amount. One person remembered 95 piastres of unpaid tithe and came up with 500 piastres. By January 10, 1972 (about twenty days after the revival began), 10,000 piastres of unpaid tithes came in.

A few people who were healed but subsequently either doubted or sinned became sick again, like Kring, who had been healed of a speech disorder. Everyone had heard him speak clearly, but because he began to doubt whether his healing would be permanent and lasting, he suddenly could not speak clearly as before.

Mrs. K'Bri, who was healed of tuberculosis and coughing blood, had regained weight and was singing in a church choir. Suddenly she became sick again after a violent argument about money with a relative. These indeed are significant lessons for the church.

Today at the writing of this account four months have passed since the beginning of the revival. The church at Dame is still in revival blessing. The church is packed out and they are joyous and zealous and full of love to each other. Also they have spread the revival blessing to many other villages. Praise God!

- By April, Helen Evans in Dalat related her eyewitness account in a letter to American donors and friends:

Easter Greetings!

The Spirit of Him who raised Jesus from the dead . . . Hallelujah! At this joyous Easter season I can assure you that this same Holy Spirit of God is transforming lives in Viet Nam, spiritually raising people from the dead!

Some of you have already heard how the Holy Spirit came down upon the student body of the Bible and Theological Institute in Nha Trang on December 3, 1971. All five of our Koho students there met the Lord in a new way, got straightened out with each other, and joyfully shared what Christ had done for them. With great anticipation we waited their return from school for Christmas vacation. We were not disappointed. In fact, God gave us a Christmas never to be forgotten.

I had the privilege of being present on December 22 when the Lord came down on the young people here in Dalat. They had presented the long-practiced program. The guests had all left and the young folks were relaxing with soda and cookies. It was about 11:30 P.M. when two of the Nha Trang students began to tell us how God had worked in their hearts. They urged their friends to confess every sin to the Lord and receive His forgiveness; then the Holy Spirit would fill them.

At first just a few started to pray quietly. Then one teenager commenced to sob as he told the Lord how he had deceived his parents and done other sinful things. I heard someone singing, "Just as I am, without one plea . . .," as he slowly made his way to the front to kneel in contrition and consecration.

Soon everyone was praying aloud, "doing business with God." Broken-hearted teenagers flung themselves at my knees, sobbing out their sins to the Lord, asking my forgiveness for certain things, and wanting me to pray with them. As various ones got everything right with God and with each other, the Holy Spirit filled them. Gradually they gravitated to the front of the church to sing and shout praises to their loving Savior. I finally came home about 3:30 A.M. but many of them remained until seven o'clock, sharing their testimonies and praising God.

The following day most of them went home for Christmas

48

in their villages. As they told what had happened to them, the Lord began to convict of sin. Adults, teenagers, and children confessed sin and experienced God's forgiveness. In a new surge of faith, the young people led the way in praying for the sick and afflicted. Countless people were healed, demons were cast out. In some churches there were unusual manifestations like a bright light shining from heaven, earth tremors; a few persons had visions. One group of young people having a prayer meeting in a grove of pines about a mile from their village heard an angelic choir singing praises to God. Some soldiers guarding a bridge nearby heard the same music.

It was very noticeable that the Christians were calling on God to do big things. In the Dangja church was an elderly man named Wor. He had a severely curved back as well as a chronic cough. One evening in a revival meeting very late he walked to the front of the church asking for prayer. "Why do you want prayer?" the pastor asked.

"For forgiveness of sin and the healing of the body."

They gathered round for prayer and the pastor commanded him to stand up straight in the name of Jesus. He tried but he couldn't.

Then the pastor asked him if he indeed believed God could heal him. He said he did. Now the pastor and many people gathered around him and again commanded him to stand up straight. The man said his back felt much better.

Finally a third time prayer was offered and he was commanded to stand up. This time he stood perfectly straight. "Hallelujah" was the first word he said. The next day many people came to Wor's house.

When he heard the story later, Missionary Tot's reaction was simply, "Is anything too hard for Jesus?" He also mentioned a noteworthy demonstration of God's power. "A Mrs. K'nga suddenly collapsed. Pastor Hui-B could not detect any life signs, so they sent for the grave clothes to prepare for burial. When Christians heard this, about twenty came to the home and began to pray. After about a half-hour she suddenly raised up. Four unbelievers came to Jesus because of this mighty work of God."

• Da Rom, Da Kab, and Da Nhan are the three churches in the Suoi Dau refugee settlement. On December 23, Kar returned from Dalat and stopped to visit at Suoi Dau. The student pastor there called a combined meeting of the three churches. Kar witnessed again about revival blessing in Indonesia, Nha Trang and Dalat. Aviong, a young man who had just experienced revival in Dalat gave his testimony and called on the young people to seek the Lord and confess their sin. Many responded to their call; weeping and confession continued until morning.

A young man named Joni renounced and turned in a fetish and another young man named Akot was healed. In many hearts burdens of sin were lifted and joy was boundless. They continued to meet and pray with all their hearts that they would be filled with God's Spirit.

Confession actually began with one of the elders named Pa Than. An older man, he and his wife were at odds and were not living together. When he stood to make his confession, people saw what appeared like a bamboo stick of fire upon his head. He also saw it, backed up, bumped into a pillar of the church building, and fell to the ground, weeping and confessing his sin. Many saw this and confessed their sin. The whole church was revived.

The Da Nhan church had experienced revival beginning December 10. Da Rom received revival December 23. Da Kab was revived last of all. Some of the Christians of the Da Kab church met with the Daromb church on the twenty-third when revival fell upon them. Many people confessed sin every night. From the twenty-fourth to the twenty-seventh eleven people renounced fetishes of every kind and fifteen people were healed of many diseases.

A strange phenomenon occurred here and then

spread to the other two churches. Altogether, twenty-five people suddenly passed out in the service as they were praying. Their unconsciousness sometimes lasted up to seven hours. During this time they experienced visions. For the most part these visions had clear spiritual and edifying content. In a few cases the meaning was unclear.

In the following days this phenomenon also occurred at six other places: Kondo Dame, Kondo Dangja, Kosi, Rhang Tot, Dam Rong, and Baoloc. Some people fell unconscious because they were resisting God and refused to confess their sin. When they revived, they publicly confessed their sin. Others confessed their sin and fell unconscious for a long period. When they revived, they told of seeing such things as a city filled with a strong light and people dressed in dazzling white apparel. Some saw themselves still with sin, and an angel would not allow them in the city. Most everything they saw was in keeping with the Scriptures. In a few cases, apparently evil spirits took advantage for what they saw did not agree with Scripture.

In summary, at the Suoi Dau settlement around eight hundred Christians were revived in the three churches. Many families were reunited with reconciliation and happiness. The church services were packed and exuberant. Every evening and morning there were prayer meetings. Many people on their own accord went out to witness.

• The church at Jong Lo is the most beautiful church building in the southern tribal district. But it was never more beautiful than at Christmastime and after when God sent revival. "Faithfully, for two years this church never missed one morning of prayer," Rev. Pah-A told us. "Now our prayers are answered."

And how! From December 24, 1971, to January 1, 1972, every Christian in the church confessed sin and repented before the Lord. Many backsliders far from the Lord came back and now are eager to meet and pray freely and spontaneously. Many sick were healed.

• The church of Da Ka is well-known to Americans since it was highlighted in Homer Dowdy's book, *The Bamboo Cross*. Many pastors and evangelists from America have since visited and ministered here. "However," said Pastor Ha Kar, "though we have had many famous American preachers and doctors of theology preach to us, we never experienced the blessing of God like we did during the revival."

Revival began on Christmas morning. Pastor Ha Kar delivered a simple, short sermon with the text, "Jesus said to him, 'Have I been so long with you yet you have not come to know Me, Philip?'" (John 14:9). He also quoted John 14:27, 28, Romans 6:13, 14, and Acts 2:1-4 and then called them to confess their sin and seek the fullness of the Holy Spirit.

God used this simple presentation in an unusual way. More than a hundred fifty people wept and confessed sin and made reconciliation with each other. From Christmas Day to December 31 the church continued to meet day and night to confess both to the Lord and to each other, correcting everything which was not pleasing to the Lord.

During these days at Da Ka:

1. Everyone, old and young, small and large, men and women and children confessed their sin, received forgiveness and hearts full of exploding joy.

2. While they were all kneeling, weeping and confessing sin to the Lord in prayer after the Christmas morning service, a Mrs. K'Truh opened her eyes and saw what appeared like sticks of fire shining upon the heads of everyone.

3. The evening of Christmas and all the evenings and mornings after that the church gathered to sing praises to God. Unbelievers in the surrounding villages later came and told the people that on these evenings they

saw what appeared to be a great light shining above the village of the Christians. People in a nearby area also said they heard something like an earthquake and were all very much afraid.

4. On the night of December 29 while Rev. Ha Kar and Sao-A were praying with people making confession of sin, suddenly the whole church saw a flash of light in the church resembling a flash bulb. On the evening of December 31 while these two men were praying, many people saw fire behind their backs so that all were afraid their clothes would ignite.

5. Sins both great and small were all confessed. Even small children five and six years old confessed things like disobeying their parents or stealing fruit from someone's garden. Many fetishes were turned in. In one case the father of a pastor brought a small ivory case used as a fetish which had been passed on from generations as far back as 300 years. Truly the power of God gained a great victory here.

6. Many were healed of diseases after they confessed their sin and prayer was made for them. Many nominal Christians and backsliders came back to the Lord. Thirty-four came and accepted the Lord.

7. Sixty-five young people together climbed a nearby mountain to pray. After a noon lunch they heard someone singing in the distance, "When I See the Blood" and also the hallelujah chorus. They ran to the area from which they heard this, but wherever they went the singing would move away from them. They saw no one. They returned around five o'clock. Later that evening they were talking to some military men who were guarding a bridge nearby. They said that they also had heard singing beginning about six-thirty and had simply assumed it was the young people still up in the mountains.

8. Around a hundred eighty young people went to a different mountain to study the Bible and pray. After a combined Bible study, they divided into groups of five to go and pray. One such group of six young men (Wan, Hak, Joi, Yai, En and Mlang) went to an area further away and knelt around a large rock. They cried out to the Lord for the hard, cold hearts of the Chru clan in that valley.

While praying, Wan put his face upon the rock. Then he heard a cracking sound. At first he paid no attention and continued to pray, but suddenly there was another crack. He opened his eyes and saw what appeared like smoke and dust rising from the stone.

He looked and saw the rock had cracked a large splinter about five centimeters long. That piece was also splintered into many smaller pieces. The fellows continued to pray, believing this was a sign that God would indeed break the hard hearts of the Chru clan.

(These young men went out to witness in many places, both in churches and to the unbelievers. Many other young people swelled their band to as many as twenty-one. After three months of weekend witnessing they had visited ten churches, and 142 Christians had made dedication of their lives. They prayed for four sick people who were healed. One leprous man was made clean. They prayed with thirty-three for salvation. Today they still are active in their ministry.)

9. About six o'clock in the evening when this large group of young people were descending from the mountain, a man in another village saw a great light shining on the group. When they crossed the road, cars on both sides stopped because they also saw the light upon the young people.

10. The two pastors' wives at Da Ka had been feuding for over ten years. But the Spirit of God worked, and

they confessed their sin to God and to each other. In order to show this new love, one of the women purchased an expensive blanket and gave it to the other.

11. One lady confessed to the church and to her husband the sin of adultery. Tribal custom demands a very severe punishment. But when the husband saw her weeping confession and that she didn't hide anything, the Spirit moved on him too and he joined his wife, kneeling in prayer until peace came to both.

- Four Vietnamese students from the Nha Trang seminary traveled to another tribal area called Bao Loc.

January 2, 1972. The four students set out for Bao Loc by bus. Praying for a sign of the Lord concerning the trip, they asked that they might be able to lead someone to the Lord during the bus trip. They did — very quickly. He was a 20-year-old tribesman and a translator for the American Special Forces. After he received Christ, they learned that he was a brother to Pastor K'Bong of the tribal church there.

Pastor Hieu took the boys over to meet the tribal pastor in the area, Pastor K'Bong. An evening meeting was arranged. After a few songs and before any of the students spoke, Pastor K'Bong began to pray.

After praying only a few words he broke down and wept. His body began to shake out of control and fell to the floor. He began to confess the sin of hard feelings toward the local Vietnamese missionary, Mr. Xuyen. He confessed to beating his wife. His eyes were closed as he lay there confessing his sin. Xuyen tried to help him up, but snapped back. "His hand is like an electric charge!" he said.

After some time, Pastor K'Bong stood up and called the church to pray for his parents. For over twenty years they had refused to believe the gospel. He sent someone to call his parents to the church. When they arrived, K'Bong prayed for them and pointed out their sinful lives. They both fell to their knees, crying out to the Lord for forgiveness. After this, K'Bong sent someone to call the parents of his wife, who had also turned a deaf ear to the gospel for years. Again, when they came to the meeting they were struck with conviction and accepted Christ.

Now the whole congregation was under great conviction. Person after person confessed specific sin.

K'Bong's young brother, who had bitterly opposed the gospel, repented. Then he told why.

"As my brother lay prostrate in prayer, I saw two people in white clothes standing on each side of him!"

This meeting would have continued on and on, but because the area was communist, they had to be in their homes by 11:00 P.M.

When they went home, at least three people who had refused to confess their sins suddenly lost consciousness. Both Pastor K'Bong and a doctor were called to the home of one lady by her husband. The doctor wanted to give her a shot to revive her . K'Bong refused, saying then she would surely never regain consciousness. He prayed for her and she revived immediately. She confessed her sin and was graciously restored to the Lord.

January 3. At 3:00 P.M. the students went to a local tribal primary school. After they testified, the children began to weep and cry, one after another crowding to the front to pray. They confessed stealing money and books. Many went to their rooms to get stolen items and return them. They went to their teachers asking forgiveness for their wrongs. One teacher, a Buddhist, prayed for salvation.

After the meeting they returned to the pastor's house. A young girl came with a heavy heart asking prayer for her parents who were not Christian. She then went home to confess sin to her parents and witness to them. That evening, before the church doors were open for the meeting, this girl brought her parents who were ready to receive Christ.

January 4. Mr. Xuyen, the Vietnamese missionary to the tribes people in this area, drove the students to a tribal village called Da Won. The church there began a meeting at 10:00 A.M. which continued until 4:00 P.M.

without a break. The whole church repented and was revived. The people brought a small child who was unconscious and near death and whose body was cold. Vinh and Thuan prayed for the child, and as they held her they could feel warmth flow back into her body.

Another lady called the whole church to pray for her husband. In one great voice, the revived Christians prayed for him. Suddenly they saw a man running from a distance. It was this husband, who asked to pray and receive Christ. He later said that suddenly there came upon him an irresistable urge to go to the church and pray. Vinh and Thuan asked the people around four o'clock if they weren't hungry. No, they wanted to continue to meet.

January 6. The students returned to Bao Loc. The Holy Spirit told Pastor K'Bong to go to another village called Dinh Quan about ninety kilometers away. Cuong and Ving also felt led to go along. The tribal Christians here lived among people who were known far and wide for their great addiction to rice alcohol and their fighting. The church was in a low spiritual state.

Cuong and Vinh began to witness. First the pastor wept and confessed how he was about to leave the church in discouragement. Then the deacon confessed to stealing money from the church treasury. Then followed a young person in the church who confessed to misappropriating church funds. Pastor K'Bong said later that he saw a white light descend on this young person as he confessed his sin.

January 7. The students now made their way back to school — three days late.

• On February 12, 1972, Jimmy, son of Pastor Sau-A along with a Mnong pastor's son from Ban Me Thuot, went to witness in a church in a Mnong village. The 800 professing Christians there were hardly different from the unbelievers even though they met faithfully on Sundays.

But when they began to call on the Lord in repentance, 400 of the heathen came and called on the Lord, even though previously they didn't know how to pray.

Thus, the church went from 800 to 1,200, and 120 people were baptized.

- Missionary Tot gave the following summary:

In the southern tribal district from December 20 to April 8, 80 churches were revived, 9,314 people made public confession of sin, 761 people surrendered fetishes, 146 people were healed, 6 insane people were delivered, a paralyzed child walked again, and one man with a curved back walks straight.

Today, although some churches have cooled off, the majority remain in revival blessing.

• Among the thirty or so tribal groups in South Viet Nam, the northernmost is the Bru. Their center is the now-famous Khe Sanh, where a U.S. Marine firebase was surrounded by North Vietnamese troops for many months. Here also was the jumping-off spot for the Vietnamese army in their ill-fated Laos incursion.

Work among these people has been in progress nearly twenty years. One of the first native workers in the small church among the Bru was a man named Chup.

In 1969 two young Bru men, Mondo and Pa Than, attended the Bible seminary in Nha Trang. Their ability in Vietnamese was limited; actually, they were auditing students. But after one year they returned to work among their people and became two very significant Christian leaders. This was especially needful, because both American and Vietnamese missionaries had been forced to leave the war-torn area.

In the 1971-72 school year, with the help and encouragement of Rev. and Mrs. John Miller, another Bru man came to study at Nha Trang. His name was Tam. It was quickly evident to me at the seminary that this young man was a God-appointed worker to his own people.

When the revival broke, the first days Tam remained quite silent. But on Sunday morning he suddenly strode to the pulpit and asked to make public confession of sin.

He asked Pastor and Mrs. Loc's young son who had lived with his parents at Khe Sanh and knew the Bru language, to interpret for him; apparently he felt a little inadequate in Vietnamese.

He declared without hesitation that he had five sins to confess: (1) gambling, (2) stealing clothes from the missionary, (3) partaking in an assassination raid into Laos, (4) stealing chickens, and (5) secretly offering food from his wedding feast to the spirits before the American and Vietnamese missionaries arrived.

During the Christmas holidays, when most of the other students went home to witness, he remained at the campus. An even more important holiday in Viet Nam is the celebration of Tet, the Chinese lunar new year. At Tet, Tam and Wan, the Koho young man whom God used so greatly to bring revival at Dalat, teamed together and returned to the Bru people to share revival.

God greatly used them. And in a matter of days after revival came to the Bru church, North Vietnamese invaded. Khe Sanh fell almost immediately, and even today it has not been retaken. God's revival was just on time.

From there Tam and Wan went to see the many Bru refugees around the city of Hue. Mrs. John Miller, one of the Wycliffe translators forced to leave Khe Sanh earlier and resettle in Hue, remembers that

> the confession of sin was continual. Sometimes, many days after the revival had come, believers would suddenly remember additional sin and immediately confess it.
>
> A little later Tam and Wan went up into the mountains of Cam Lo and here the Lord also worked in a great way. There were not many believers there, but they confessed sin and many unbelievers were converted.
>
> From here Tam and Wan went up to Cua, which is the largest concentration of Bru. They met with Christians from afternoon till eleven at night. They planned to meet again the next morning at seven, but by five o'clock the people had already gathered. They met steadily till 5:00 P.M.
>
> What surprised the Bru themselves was that no one became hungry all day. There was much confession of sin. Fetishes which had been kept for years were surrendered, and many were healed.
>
> Pa Than's father was partially blind; he could see light, but he could not recognize anyone. The Lord healed him.
>
> A girl whose hand had been crippled and useless from the time she was a year or two old was healed in answer to prayer. A little later she couldn't move her hand again. So

they prayed a second time and it now remained active.

That night this girl and other teenage girls who were sleeping together were awakened by a light. This girl got up and she began to pray in fluent Vietnamese. The other girls were startled and awed, so they began to pray in Bru. (Most tribes people do not speak Vietnamese but recognize it). They prayed till 4:00 A.M., and then went to sleep. The next morning they asked the girl to pray again in Vietnamese, but she could only pray in Bru.

Nuan, our Bru houseboy, had become a believer not too long before he came to us, and was quite interested in spiritual things. However, he had a very bad home background and was subject to moods. Therefore, we were sorry — but not completely surprised — when he did not get excited about the revival.

Our girl worker was the opposite — just bubbling over about the Lord and what He was doing. She told Nuan about it, but he didn't seem at all interested. Then we found out why. "I can't sleep or eat," he said. "It seems like there are two people inside of me. One wants me to go along with this revival and the other just laughs at all this and makes me feel embarrassed."

I told him that in a time of revival this is the way it is. Either you are happy because the Holy Spirit gives you joy, or you are very miserable. After we finished eating I suggested Nuan and I go over to Pastor Mondo's house. Surprisingly, Nuan agreed. So we went and found that Tam and Wan had already left and gone up to Cam Lo and Cua. Mondo was there, so I told him about how Nuan was so unhappy and asked if he would pray with Nuan so he could know God's peace and joy in his heart. Mondo decided we had better pray right then, rather than wait for Tam and Wan. So we gathered around with Chup and his wife, who were also there.

Mondo and Chup had been at odds, but now they were bubbling over in love. Mondo's wife and mother and little brother were also there. We read a passage of Scripture and then everyone began to pray at once.

Mondo asked Nuan if he had confessed his sin and he made some kind of negative response. Then I heard Mondo pray for Nuan, asking God to help him confess his sin. When I opened my eyes I saw that Nuan had suddenly fallen on the floor, and Mondo was yelling: "Oh! God! Nuan is dying."

(*Passing out* and *dying* are the same word in Bru). "Lord, help him to confess his sins!"

The noise and commotion had reached some Vietnamese who lived out in the back. They came to the door and saw Nuan lying helpless on the floor. They were very disturbed. "Don't you think he should be taken to the hospital?" somebody said.

We just nodded and went on praying. It was a terrifying experience. He was completely out; there was no response. We all prayed earnestly that the Lord would help Nuan and bring him back and cast the evil spirit out of him.

We continued praying, but he didn't regain consciousness. Still we prayed, but with no response.

For some reason, Mondo spoke up:

"What's your name?"

"Fear," answered Nuan very clearly, and then shook all over for about a minute or so. I had my hand on him and I could feel him shaking.

They continued to pray. Chup was holding his head. He started talking to Nuan.

"Pray after me." Nuan sort of grunted three times as if he heard. After a while, I appealed directly to him.

"Nuan! What do you feel?"

"I don't feel anything."

"Can you pray?"

There was no response.

Then Mondo said, "Pray after me," and this time he prayed the prayer of the penitent sinner, asking the Lord to forgive him.

Nuan prayed this after Mondo until Mondo mentioned the name of the devil. Then Nuan stopped praying.

"Say it! Nuan!" Mondo ordered. And finally Nuan did. Then Mondo told him to pray:

"Cast the devil out of me, Lord."

Nuan would not say it.

Mondo challenged him three times to pray, and finally he did.

Then I asked Nuan how he felt. He replied, "A little warm." I suggested that he pray and thank the Lord for what He had done and ask Him to complete His work in his heart. He prayed a few phrases. I asked him again how he felt, and he replied, "A little warmer."

Then it seemed like the floodgate broke loose and he burst into tears, weeping and praying and asking God to help him. Mondo asked him how he felt when they had begun to pray for him. He said he had just had a great urge to jump up and run away. He had no memory whatever of the period while he was unconscious, nor of the time he had prayed after Mondo.

From that day on, Nuan was a new person in our house. He was so open and loving. It was a complete change in his personality. It's so thrilling for us to see how the Lord is blessing him and how he wants to know the Lord more.

● In other words, the revival continues. It is long-standing. In Cua they are still meeting. Pa Than says there are now four hundred people there who really know·the Lord, and anyone of them could lead others to know Him. He said that no matter where the North Vietnamese might take them or into how many groups they may be split up, there will be somebody who knows the Lord.

Before the revival he wasn't sure that any of them could have stood the test of trouble and persecution. So we thank the Lord for this blessing.

Part Three
In Life and in Death

Viet Nam — *however else it may be viewed* — *is a land of death. Funerals have become regular events in the lives of almost everyone. It is estimated that since 1961 the war alone has taken more than 1.1 million military lives. And who knows how many civilians have died?*

The revival — *an invasion of spiritual life* — *has had its effect on dying in Viet Nam. The following two chapters illustrate what I mean. To Y'Djhang the Holy Spirit granted a dramatic resurrection from the dead. In My Dung's case, the Lord has given to her family and fiance the strength and courage to go on while she enjoys the wonders of heaven. With the Apostle Paul I am grateful that through "prayers and the provision of the Spirit . . . Christ shall even now, as always, be exalted . . . whether by life or by death" (Philippians 1:19,20).*

7

Y'Djhang's Pile of Gold

Y'Tang was the language teacher of Hank Blood, the Wycliffe missionary captured in the 1968 Tet offensive and starved to death in a jungle prison. Mr. Blood had witnessed to Y'Tang and prayed many months that the Lord would save him and use him as an instrument to reach his tribe.

It was not until a district conference in the spring of 1971 that Y'Tang heard a message and felt called into the ministry. He then determined to go to Bible school and prepare himself to take the gospel to the Mnong people.

However, being a very gifted young man with a high-school education, the government tempted him to take a teaching position in one of the tribal schools. He decided not to go to Bible school. Shortly after, Y'Tang's younger brother died very suddenly.

This led Y'Tang to repent and renew his desire to go to Bible school, only to be confronted by another offer from the government — this time to work in the provincial office for ethnic minorities. "Here's an opportunity to help my people," he rationalized. So he accepted the position. Then his younger sister suddenly dropped dead.

Y'Tang sent a letter to the Ban Me Thuot Bible School informing them that he was enrolling for studies. After only three months of training he was sent to a village to be a student pastor. The Lord had spoken to his heart when Jimmy Sau ministered at the Bible school. At that time even the young people in the high-school hostel were praying morning, afternoon, and evening, singing late into the night.

Coming from this revival, Y'Tang returned to his village. There he found his church members mourning and carrying on like the heathen because someone had died. Many of his own Christians were even eating food offered to the dead. He rebuked them, and the Lord began to speak through him to his people.

Before long, two of his leading deacons got up and wanted to confess sin. But soon Y'Tang interrupted one of them.

"Look, you're not confessing the right sins."

"What do you mean?"

"You have ruined the lives of two women." Immediately the Lord told Y'Tang the names of the women. The man fell on his face to repent and confess his sin.

The second deacon began to confess. Again, Y'Tang stopped him.

"You are not confessing the right sins. You too have ruined the lives of two women." After the deacon denied it, Y'Tang said, "The Lord has told me the names of those women," and he proceeded to call them.

The deacon was deeply convicted of his sin and repented. From there the revival spread throughout the church.

According to Y'Tang, on February 14, 1972, a total of forty-six adults, eighty-four young people, and over two hundred children prayed and confessed their sins. He cast out demons in the name of Christ, and prayer continued until 3:30 A.M. Many of the villagers came to see what was happening, for the outbursts of confession, prayer, and praise had gotten so noisy that they were afraid the communists would hear them.

Although there are other stories of raisings from the dead, the most unusual one took place in the early morning of May 12, 1972.

A young man by the name of Y'Djhang from the village of Lac Thien, about fourteen or fifteen years of age, had died from a heart ailment of long standing. The worst part was that he had died immediately after another student pastor, Y'Pong, had given him a shot of penicillin. The parents naturally blamed Y'Pong very bitterly, who didn't know what else to do, so he fell on his knees and prayed, asking the Lord to help him.

He prayed from midnight until two A.M., then ran to call Y'Tang to pray with him. The key verse in their praying was, "He Himself bore our sins in His body on the cross, that we might die to sin and live to righteousness; for by His wounds you were healed" (I Peter 2:24). They sang "There is Power in the Blood" over and over again. Fifteen times they read the Bible, prayed and sang, but the boy did not come back to life.

What happened thereafter is best told by Y'Tang himself:

> Then I was discouraged and very sad, especially when the dead boy's mother began to wail.
> "Do you believe that your child can live?" I asked.
> "Yes, I believe it."

So I told her, "If you really believe your child will live again, then stop your wailing and leave alone the clothing and dishes you're preparing for burial." Then I did as Paul did to Eutychus; I picked Y'Djhang up and began to pray. I couldn't lift him by myself so I asked three other fellows to help me. I prayed with all my heart in the Mnong language. A crowd began to gather to watch. But nothing happened. So we put the boy back down.

Y'Pong was getting more edgy by the minute, until I said: "Oh, Jesus Christ, if you have chosen me to work among Mnong Rolom to save my people, then give me a sign. The sign that I want is that this boy shall live or, if he can't come back to life, then You let me die and take his place because You have died to take my place. I will take this boy's place in death that he may live and Your name might be glorified."

I didn't pray any more. I just used the name of Christ. I grabbed hold of the dead boy's hand and said:

"In the name of Jesus of Nazareth, oh, Y'Djhang, get up."

His waist began to pop up and down. Then, he bent at the waist and sat up. Every time I used the name of Christ his fingers began to twitch, so I knew he was going to live. Again I used the name of the Lord Jesus, and in a little while he was able to breathe. When he began, I was filled with fear: it was as though his breath came from his stomach and gurgled up. That happened a number of times, and then he began to breathe properly.

Next I asked Y'Pong to pray, using the name of Jesus, to open the boy's eyes. His eyes opened, but he couldn't see anything. The mother was really frightened. She saw that her child's eyes could only stare. Y'Pong used the name of Christ so that the boy's hands and feet moved properly. Then we asked the Lord again to heal his eyes, which He did.

God had raised him! His body was soft and warm, and he was breathing again.

After that we rested for a while, waiting for the family to come back from the rice fields. And that was an opportunity for us to open the Word of God to John 3:16 and preach it to the boy's father and mother — but to no avail.

When his whole family arrived I had them all gather around Y'Pong. All the unbelievers stood on one side and all the believers stood over by me and we sang, "Hallelujah, Praise the Lord." That was about six o'clock. Then I prayed once more:

"I thank the Lord because You have returned the soul of Y'Djhang. Only right now let him be able to speak and tell us everything that has happened to him. I turn him over to You. Amen." The onlookers then gasped, for as soon as the amen had been said, Y'Djhang got up immediately, almost bumping into me as he arose.

He put his hands out and said, "Oh, mother, where is my gold?" He repeated this two more times. Then he looked over to his left side and saw me. I told him, "The power of God has given you a reward for your faith. Right now the Lord has given you back your soul. You and I, let's sing, 'Hallelujah, Praise the Lord.'"

But he couldn't speak because his jaw was stiff. We got a spoon to open his mouth. We couldn't budge it. I then asked his mother to take a cloth and dip it in hot water and put it over his mouth. At the end he could speak, "Hallelujah."

That evening was a service. I used Acts 2:27 as my text. I asked again that the Lord would pour out His Spirit upon us. After the service I went over to Y'Djhang's house. It was about eight-thirty and about a thousand people, believers and unbelievers, were waiting to hear what Y'Djhang had to say. It was obvious that he was still sick. However, he said, "What happened to me is forbidden for unbelievers. I can only tell this to believers." So I asked that he be carried to the church.

Y'Djhang commenced to tell a fantastic story. He had seen a broad road jammed with multitudes of people slowly making their way to the brink of hell. Then in heaven he had been shown his mansion, which was yet in construction. But to his disappointment, he found that there was only a small pile of gold on a bare table in the house. A voice said to him, "This is your house. You have built this with the things you have offered on earth. If you offer a little bit, you are going to reap a little bit. If you offer a lot, you are going to reap a lot." Then the voice said, "Now you can go back home because you haven't sent up enough things."

Y'Djhang replied, "I don't want to go back even though I don't have enough; I want to stay here." However, he was told that many people were calling him back to earth and that he had to return there even though one day he would be able to come back to his house in heaven.

One of the most unexplainable things was that the Lord taught him a song which he had never heard before and which had never been sung in his village. It was an old

French tune, number 166 in the Raday hymnbook. He was told that when he returned to earth he was to preach on Acts 2:27 and sing this particular hymn. Strangely enough, he was able to stand up and spontaneously sing this hymn.

Since he was raised from the dead, 140 people have newly believed in the Lord. Some of the church leaders have visited Y'Djhang's village and testified that the church is crowded out. Twenty-two people were baptized on the one Sunday that Mr. Cung and Mr. Y'Ngue visited.

Mr. Y'Ngue is a highly respected district superintendent of the Raday tribal church around Ban Me Thuot. He and, for that matter, the entire Raday church have accepted this account as factual. Mr. Y'Ngue took Y'Tang and Y'Djhang on a tour of Raday churches so they could testify of this marvelous act of God's power. Great spiritual blessing and victories followed their speaking.

Miss Mildred Ade, a missionary nurse for many years, was living in Ban Me Thuot at the time. She soon interviewed Y'Tang and taped his account. Her medical opinion, as stated to me: "Y'Djhang had been very sick with heart trouble for some days. When injected with penicillin, he went into anaphylactic shock, and then he was gone. It was quite some time before prayer was offered."

It should be said that there were no medically trained people to take Y'Djhang's blood pressure and pronounce him dead. If, however, we can believe the eyewitnesses, he had stopped breathing for quite some time and the family had begun to prepare for the burial. Furthermore, if we can believe Y'Tang, the return of breathing was very observable.

Those of us who believe that the power of the name of Christ is ample to perform this phenomenon will surely accept the aggregate of the data. We praise God

for His demonstrated power to His church and unbelievers alike. Others will surely try to find natural
causes for this event. But we might remember that there
were no proper medical authorities to pronounce the
Son of God dead at Golgotha, either. We are left to the
veracity of the eyewitnesses of the Cross.

No matter how you look upon this event, it proved to
be an instrument in God's program to advance His
Kingdom.

The Christian and Missionary Alliance missionaries
in Viet Nam accept the account at face value. Field
Chairman Stebbins included the following in his
official annual report:

> One missionary writes regarding the effect of revival at
> Ban Me Thuot: "While such miraculous events as healing,
> angelic choirs, visions, a number of enemy sightings of
> soldiers in white guarding Christian villages, and *one docu-
> mented raising from the dead* occurred, the major emphasis has
> been outreach to the lost. Early-morning and late-hour prayer
> meetings have been the common thing." Hundreds of new
> believers have been added to the church and new churches
> have been opened.

The revival has continued on. Doubt has turned into
expectancy, pride has been humbled, sin has been confessed. Wherever there is criticism, doubt, and holding
back, the revival has been quenched or has not come at
all. Its chief characteristics have been prayer, public
confession of sin, the filling of the Holy Spirit, boundless joy, daring faith, various miracles, and a bold witness. The maturity of the revival is shown in that *miracles have not been sought.* They have occurred only as
the people got right with God and the Lord chose to
send such miracles. Healings, however, have been
sought and secured through faith.

8

Massacre at Que Son

In 1962 when we first arrived in Viet Nam, we began language study in Da Nang. We were assigned an apartment adjacent to the home of Rev. Nguyen Xuan Vong, the Vietnamese district superintendent of the North Central District of the Evangelical Church of Viet Nam. Among his sons was a spirited teenager named Tin. During those years in Da Nang he became known as a foe of the American missionaries. He was very good at discrediting and embarrassing us.

Upon our return to Viet Nam in 1969, after a furlough, we were assigned to teach at the Nha Trang institute. We had hardly put down our bags when a group of young fellows whom we had known in Da Nang came to greet us. They were all older now, students preparing for the ministry. Among them, surprisingly, was Tin.

He told me his story. He had gotten considerably involved in subversive politics, renounced the family faith and embarrassed his father. Then Rev. Tom Stebbins happened to be in the Da Nang church, and Tin happened to attend. The convicting power of the Holy Spirit pierced his heart and he was born again. Now with God's call clear in his mind he was preparing for the ministry.

The next summer he, with the others in his class, were assigned to two-year student pastorates. Tin accepted the call to Chien Dang, an area well behind enemy control. After two years he returned for further training at the Bible institute. We discerned a dark attitude in Tin which continued until the revival broke in December 1971. God moved into his life.

Later, he told how that just a few days before the revival he had launched a secret movement to try to force all missionaries out of the land. Besides his double-agentry, he confessed many other sins. He said that while in the pastorate he had received some money from a missionary and had used only a part of it for its designated purpose, pocketing the rest.

That very afternoon this missionary arrived to visit the school. I was present when Tin gave him a Seiko watch to pay the money he owed.

As the revival continued at the school, Tin and the others in my class on revival were suddenly thrust into leadership roles. Tin proved to have the dynamic qualities needed. It was he who made a fiery call for additional repentance in the Sunday morning worship service in front of many Vietnamese faculty members who were dubious about the revival. Tin, along with Ha and Thien, were also among those who went out to Vietnamese churches and shared the revival.

As the 1972 school year drew to a close, Tin came to me and shared his desire to spend the summer months traveling with a band of young people, sharing revival and preaching to the unconverted. To do this, he had to turn down a lucrative job offer and simply go by faith concerning the next year's tuition.

In June we left for a year of furlough. For months I didn't hear from Tin, until one day I received word from a missionary that, in an attack at Que Son, Tin's fiancee was killed. In the November 22, 1972, issue of the *Alliance Witness,* the following account appeared:

To those for whom the battle was more than a newspaper headline, Que Son was an acid test which validated the revival that had earlier brought new vitality to so much of the highlands of northern South Vietnam.

Most Americans dismissed the "heavy fighting" in the area of Que Son as just one more skirmish in the long and costly Vietnam war.

To Rev. Nguyen Van Sy, pastor of the Evangelical Church (C&MA) in that town, and to his prospective son-in-law, Pastor Nguyen Xuan Tin, a fifth-year student at Nha Trang Biblical and Theological Institute, it was personal and heartrending.

Rev. and Mrs. Woodford Stemple, missionaries at Da Nang, translated these eyewitness reports which so graphically portray the tragedy and triumph of Viet Nam today.

Pastor Tin, the fifth-year student at Nha Trang, begins:

"Wednesday, August 16, my father, the district superintendent, gave me a letter and an application form for the Nha Trang Bible Institute so that my fiancee, My Dung, (pronounced *Me Yoom),* could complete it in time to enter school."

"Thursday, August 17, I went to Que Son to see My Dung, arriving at 11:00 A.M. Firebase Ross, two meters from the church, was under rocket attack which had begun earlier in the morning and lasted until noon.

"After lunch My Dung filled in her application for the school. All details for entering school had been cared for by our parents. We had plane tickets for flying to Nha Trang on September 7.

"I left Que Son at three o'clock to return to Da Nang, where my mother was to have major surgery the next day. The date of surgery had been advanced from the 22nd to the 18th. Otherwise I would have remained in Que Son overnight."

Here Pastor Sy takes up the story:

"Thursday night we had a cottage prayer meeting near the Que Son church in the home of Mrs. Cuu. After the meeting I talked at length with My Dung, my daughter, advising her of things she would need to know when she left for Bible school.

"About midnight we heard rifle fire. Early the next morning the Viet Cong appeared near the church. Planes began to bomb them. All the houses in the neighborhood, including those of the Christians, were burned, with the exception of the church and parsonage. The people who were still alive, Christians and non-Christians, ran to the parsonage for refuge, about sixty or seventy people.

"That evening at about six o'clock two bombs fell next to the parsonage. The church, the parsonage, and the youth meeting hall collapsed completely. About thirty people were killed. All the rest were injured, some seriously.

"About ten minutes later the Lord led the church treasurer, who had taken shelter about three hundred meters away, to run to the church to remove the beams and bricks from those who were trapped, including my wife, myself, and our children. It pleased the Lord that two of our children, My Dung (nineteen years) and My Duc (fourteen years), should return to Him.

"The church treasurer carried my wife, who was seriously wounded, to the house of a Christian near the district center. I was wounded in the leg and face. Our other children were also wounded.

"That night we slept at the home of the Christian where my wife had been taken. The man's family had already left. Bombs were falling in the surrounding area. Nearly all the houses were burned.

"Although I was wounded, I concerned myself during the night with giving medical help to my wife and other Christians, using the few bandages and medicines which I had carried with me when we fled.

"On Saturday, August 19, they carried my wife to the district center to try to get her evacuated by helicopter. Because the place was being rocketed, no planes could land. Firebase Ross nearby had been abandoned.

"In the afternoon our soldiers also abandoned the district center. All day we searched for an escape route but we could find none. Finally Christians carried my wife to the house of a believer who lived near a mountain where we spent the night."

Back in Da Nang, Pastor Tin, watching over his mother who had just undergone surgery, had no word of the capture of Que Son until Saturday. He takes up the story again:

"I hurried to Huong An, the area on the main highway nearest Que Son. There I discovered the three youngest children in My Dung's family who, with the church secretary, had been able to escape Que Son. I learned that my fiancee and her younger sister had returned to be with the Lord and that my prospective father-in-law and mother-in-law, Mr. and Mrs. Sy, had been wounded. I took the three children back to Da Nang and that afternoon returned by car to Huong An, taking with me my father (the district superintendent) and my brother-in-law, Pastor Que. There we received the word (erroneous) that Mrs. Sy had died. We returned in great sadness to Da Nang. My father and I knelt to pray through the whole night."

Meanwhile, back at Que Son, Pastor Sy relates what happened:

"We met Sunday morning, August 20, at 6:00 A.M. to pray. Then my wife and I and several Christians tried again to get out. But the Viet Cong were stopping traffic at many points, so we returned by a roundabout way to the mountain.

"One of my daughters, My Lang, and another Christian girl carried my wife while I hobbled with a cane. We witnessed before our faces the death of many people, but the Lord kept us safe.

"At one point a Viet Cong drew his gun and shot in the air, but our small children hugged me and challenged: 'Our father is a pastor and he has been wounded. Please don't shoot.' The Viet Cong looked and let us go."

Pastor and Mrs. Sy and the three children with them came out at Huong An Sunday morning, August 20, at about 10:30.

They were taken to Da Nang by the Chu Lai Christian Orphanage car. Another child, Thien Ai, age seven, turned up after he had been missing for five days. Wounded in the attack on Que Son, he was first carried by a non-Christian young person and then passed along from person to person until he finally ended in the care of the church treasurer.

As of September 5, twenty-six Que Son Christians were known dead and twenty others were wounded, some seriously. Seven were captured. Fifty-seven are still unaccounted for.

After hearing only the brief news that Tin's fiancee had been killed, I received a letter from Tin himself. I shuddered to open it and learn his reactions, especially since the bombs on the church at Que Son probably came from American warplanes.

After a very factual account of the tragedy, he wrote these words:

"Missionary! I thank God that revival came to me in December of 1971.

"Surely the Lord knew the trial that awaited me. If I had not received this visitation of God first, I know that I could not hold up in this trial."

Such faith was truly in keeping with the miracles in this revival. It is obvious that hunger, disagreements, poverty, conflict, and even bombs are not going to stop it.

Tin is only one of many whom God anointed during the revival. Countless others will never be the same. And in the years ahead, the church in Viet Nam will never be the same.

In Viet Nam, there will always be a war. Not a war of guns and napalm and political wrangling, I hope.

But there will always be a spiritual war. For there is a new type of soldier in Viet Nam. He is the Christian soldier. A soldier who has proved his superior firepower in the form of Jesus Christ and does not hesitate to call upon Him to annihilate Satan.

God is still in Viet Nam!